PRUDENCE
BUSSEY-CHAMBERLAIN
(COTERIES.)

NEWTON-LE-WILLOWS

Published in the United Kingdom in 2018
by The Knives Forks And Spoons Press,
51 Pipit Avenue,
Newton-le-Willows,
Merseyside,
WA12 9RG.

ISBN 978-1-912211-15-9

Acknowledgements:

'Prologue' was published in issue 5 of *Hysteria*.

The cover photo is by Kimberley Bussey-Chamberlain and the cover was designed
by Elke Bussey.

Supported using public funding by

ARTS COUNCIL
ENGLAND

CONTENTS

Prologue

We are all worried about non-consensual
urine   & the things that look   like
non-consensual urine.   Wilfully obtuse
together   me angled over   your nose
bridging the gap of brushed denim crotch
between us   I think
of your nose & loneliness
                    crude, unchanging blues
Winter

They can't breathe in Ferguson   &
between my thighs you are struggling too
          we are esprit & broken glasses
          Netflix direct to television   a free
burrito with every Christmas jumper

Knee deep in everything, which are only news
outlets online   we perform uncensored;
all we want is to ejaculate on screen
          & to live without fear.

Somewhere, Russell Brand eats a pasty,
somewhere, we all have appetites, &
everywhere we are becoming skilled
iconographers, or cartographers, or
professionals on who has died where
and why it matters for a brand new hashtag

(COTERIES.)

*It's my poetic dilemma, it seems. To include the
body, mine, the woman's as I see it, to approach
this blood as part of the score. It should show
up regularly in the culture's poems, this female
conversation, because most of the poets who
write bleed every month until they pass
childbearing years. I'm waiting to watch the
room change*[1]

---

[1] Eileen Myles 'The Lesbian Poet' in *School of Fish* (Black Sparrow, 1997)

There is a dead female poet
in my pants
I suppose it was inevitable;
trading always in histories
& having pockets large
enough to hold Semiotext(e)
editions

in the dark &
handsome night
a fox screams
for a mate or fuck
but I think it could
be you calling
& I am in bed with
a carving knife
resting on my
newest chapbook

the bathroom light pales on the carpet's
resilience; living alone
is making me
shake all around my hands
I am high
on nothing
but solitude
& cheek-boned
seriousness

I am no-one
in the half-
London sun

You look like you've
spent your whole life
being beautiful

I; girl; the
international
booty call

carry my Oyster
in my pocket just
to rub against machines

I sleep with a bottle
of hot sauce; this is
no *Sex in the City*

I make abstracts
of your lineation
& careless teeth marks

I'm kissing
everywhere & this
is a disaster

This scene is so   mmm   grimy

I imagine
fucking you
astride my ring-
pull beer
          £3 a can; Red Stripe chilled
fantasy & rimming
leaving my tongue
bleeding with practice

you're not here
          almost feels painful
if I went in for viscera

these poems do nothing
for feminism;
except   I go
on marches
sleep with the women
write about it

then I betray them; sleep with men; don't write
about it
                    there is something
                    so dirty about semis &
                    colons

in the bright nights
of your own
brilliance
I like when death
kind of happens
around us but not
really

action in motion
whenever you talk

      & I don't believe in love
so at least essentialism is out
as we're not really the sexes we are
but the socially inscribed
genders realised through
the sex act
               & I want
so much that way
         confused & anti-binary; swinging &
kissing
before you've found a mouth for contact

why might you kiss > actions speak
louder than words
but
they don't
which is why
the weakness of my lyric
activism is forgivable in some ways
'I' is not pretending anymore at least

I masturbate with a Wii remote
to Mario Smash Brothers
    I have a handle
    on saleable fun & the growing
    gaming industry
& can get Mario
and Luigi tag-teaming on vibrate

Princess Peach's special
move
when you press up & - at the same
time
is to shoot flowers
from her navel

for as long as I can remember
I have narrated pushing shopping
trolleys in the supermarket like it's
figure skating; I get points for technique
grace & difficulty of manoeuvre

I saw two men robbing the
parking meter with spanners
at 3am in the morning
& I've never seen a human
move so alert with fear
of being caught
        so I stood twitching
my own curtain in suburban cliché
& did not call the police

make no plans; the avant-garde
think the world is burning down
& they are our prophets in the absence
of everything biblical
so let's stay in
or start fires in cars
depending on what time
the revolution takes off;
the wine will be iced
in the fridge for when
we get back

you are my twitter trauma
my one time kiss & run
a substance valentine August abuse
& some days I wake up looking like every
member of the Brady Bunch family

Our shame in London
is not the same as shame
in Paris   which is
honte
          & like a duck reading
Sedgwick & being eaten
by Peter's wolf
          which is Polari for those
who don't know better

I love cop dramas
so much   I have recently applied
for MI5
          because Vauxhall
is a very easy commute for me
& I am 5' 5" 7st blonde blue eyed
forgettable
                    you have to be incognito
to be a spy
          or at worst unremembered
I have a face
like everyone
I am the human average

John Wieners
described a poet as
a wraith who crosses time
not accounting for
the waif who takes-on crime;
watches *Rizzoli & Isles* on Alibi+1
          I shall be vigilante justice
for sex offenders & rape everywhere

I will wear trouser suits that
would scare even Vanessa Place
& Tragoedia shall be my middle name;
my mournful look; my crime scene bedside
manner

you don't mind popular music
but the capitalism of it all
upsets you more than the sexism

blurred lines of consumer culture
are not just Robin Thicke's problem
but ours & you have not been

to the Tate Modern recently because
you now see the beauty of abstract
expressionism as Jessie J price tags

:
we take it to Facebook email
        which is the new street encounter
my nightmare is that our
conversations will be revealed
to us as nothing

though you are left-leaning
        & do not even use text-speak
ironically

my some-time sad love
you were so collegiate once –
language *is* consciousness
what it expresses is social interest

I stand around in groups
so self-aware
when I say I like Miley Cyrus
it's kitsch-hip-commodity-
culture-critique

I really do like Miley Cyrus

what happens
when you're
giving a reading
of your avant-
garde poetry
having spent
many years
reading *Das Kapital*
in original German
& someone from
the street walks in;
someone of the
people & just
doesn't like what
you do –
they use syntax
traditionally
& have a loan
with Barclaycard

what is the
sound of one
poet reading
if only the intellig-
ensia is around
to hear it?

Eileen Myles once said
it had been a trend for a while
amongst the lady-poets
to write long poems   & she always
thought

      Why would you do that?

to say more & still nothing,
Eileen.

A VOYAGE;

A MEDITATION ON FLIPPANCY;

MY ENCOUNTERS WITH TOMATOES

A six day voyage is too long
to be literally all out at sea
when I'm such a figurative girl
           turn me like a phrase
           tongue twist me polysyllabic
           and draw me like one of your French
girls
because everyone wants
the life of Kate Winslet

           I sit in bars between two cities
I wear purple
green skinny jeans
though you rail against them:
homosexual uniform
you say, but how can I fit in
anything that is not *Less than Zero*
or some other Bret Easton Ellis
so enjoy your skirt subversion
which is only good for lifting

With your concern
for depth   x   width   x   height
and my love
of bright & shiny
surfaces
this will never work

The sexual act
of eating
tomato soup
she sits   off-centre on a bar stool
with her spoon a letter
of the alphabet
in the minestrone of dining and

living. I watch her & remember

the structuralist
way you wore
your hair
that I can be
led to a bedroom
but can't be
made to drink

RE-WRITING 50 SHADES OF GREY
FOUND TEXT IN AN ACT OF FEMINIST POETIC APPROPRIATION

The bit where Angel Clare says fuck off? Ana, so help me, where the fuck are you? Holy fuck ... he's going to kiss me. Fuck! Oh, fuck the paperwork. Firstly, I don't make love. I fuck ... hard. Fuck hard! Holy shit, that sounds so ... hot. Inquisition. Holy fuck. Punishment, the nature of which shall be determined by the Dominant. Holy Fuck. Why the fuck didn't you tell me? I thought you didn't make love. I thought you fucked hard. I'm going to fuck you now, Miss Steele. Want me to fuck you again? Holy fuck. This is wrong, but holy hell is it erotic. I want to fuck your mouth, Anastasia, and I will soon. His breathing more disjointed. 'Fuck my mouth!' I moan. His face in my hair. 'Fuck Ana'. Just-fucked hair doesn't. Me – fucking – not lovemaking – she. Just-fucked hair really, really suits him. I want to fuck your mouth. Me want to fuck you, and you're sore. His throat. Fuck my mouth. I can fuck him with my mouth. My sex. Oh fuck. Holy fuck. I cry out. His just-fucked hair. Just-fucked pigtails. I will fuck you in the elevator. Methods of pain. Holy fuck. Real mind-fuck. Perhaps. Freeze. Fuck. How shall I fuck you? I fuck you this way, or this way, or this way? I whimper. Please fuck me. He came here to fuck me. Weapon. Fuck you into submission? Love-we fuck. Trust me. I will fuck you. What I eat. How I fuck. Give a fuck. With him, he will fuck me. I stand. Fuck me in the private dining room. Poor, fucked-up, kinky. You're fucking. Fuck! All the blood. What the fuck have I done? Control not to fuck you on the hood of this car. Fucking car, I'll buy you a fucking car. Holy fuck ... me in charge. Everywhere. Fuck. I am fucking him. I am in charge. Fifty shades of fucked up. Fuck you very quick. I cannot move. Oh fuck. Holy fuck it hurts. Now I'm going to fuck you. Woman you fuck. Woman I fuck. Completely fucked up. Why is he so fucked up? What the fuck. What the fuck. Intense, fucked-up. I just want to tie you up and fuck you senseless. I want to fuck you standing up. Fifty shades of fucked up. Deeply. Holy fuck. I'm going to fuck you hard. Thoroughly fucked and in need. Holy Fuck. Fifty shades of fucked up. Spank and then fuck you. Holy fuck. To fuck you on the couch. I've taken a punishment fuck. *We've all been there.* In my just-fucked state my just-fucked hair. I will fuck you in this elevator. You'll be fucked. Don't you want to fuck? Then we'll fuck. Balls in his mouth. Fuck, this is sexier than the toothbrush. Holy fuck ... This is fucking – and I love it. I'm not saying thank you for fucking me. Fucked. Actually the fucking. Holy fuck, he's here. Me. Holy fuck. Nearby toilet. Holy fuck. Sweet mother of all. Fucked up her marriage. Holy fuck. The evil one has a name. Holy fuck – it's exciting. Holy fuck! My scalp prickles. Holy fuck ... what has he got planned that I need safewords? Or I will fuck it with you on your knees. Inside me ... oh fuck ... and I cry out again. Agonizingly slowly. Holy fuck – please! I'm screaming inside. Holy fuck – what's he going to do now? I've always wanted to fuck to it. It's the first time I've fucked. Oh fuck. Fuck! Holy fuck, this is going to hurt. You are one fucked-up son of a bitch. Fuck – this is it. Holy fuck. This really is it. Well he could have told us the fucking truth. This is a real fuck up. No, fucked, we would have fucked on the piano. It's always been fucking to him.

In New York
they take
my fingerprints my passport my retinal trace

and the USA has more
of me bodily than my
                                    cuntry
(which I just wanted to try because it's a bit
Kathy Acker)

My passport
is checked
against my face
& recognised
by my photo-
booth resentment
                        they let me in

So I can commit
No crimes here
No castrations
No jaywalking –
Vigilante feminism –
I'll have to drink coffee
and beers
Eileen Myles
and Frank O'Hara
& forget city politics for a time.

It's a shame
New York
expects something

more of me;
                    maybe I will write
something explicit
                    about masturbation
                    or Obamacare
                    after one-too-many of a
taxation-heavy beer

In this mechanised urban landscape
the accoutrement horizon is less suited
to doing it yourself;
what can you buy to do it for you
what can you do to buy it for you
can do buy you

I wait for transatlantic
phone reception
to send you
this great new
poem I rediscovered

I am in the docks of NY; I use semi-colons
                    incorrectly

& I am not a butch worker
short haired muscled
no night walker looking
for a good time sailor
but small & blonde & obsessed with the
possibilities of an American cowboy
machismo

so I wear denim. Am I
mobile or nubile or
both
blushed dawn
leg spread over
a duvet when I
wake in the morning.

I figured since she was a girl she couldn't be too
good. I mean at that time, it was that way, just to
be straight about it. She was a girl, she
wasn't somebody specific

this morning I watched
the sunrise in my pants
which is a Fire Island
dialogue of itself & last

night we heard
jazz live

my ampersands are affectation
I couldn't write them until a year ago
then I practised it; it's just like walking in
heels or being a bike

You never forget & nor does anyone else

I had one of those awful
revelations when I was
eating pizza
that all I'm theorising here is mobility
but when I tried to get up I could barely
walk for the cheese stuffed crust
& my poetics slowed up 5th
where I was lost but saw the Empire State
building a whole new sense of place
around the Olson pace of my feet;

I use my sister's
Dumb blond© hair product

I use my sister's
Lancôme© eye-liner sharpener for my pencil

I use my sister's
inflated sense of self

I use my sister's
historical feminist resonance

I use my sisters'
historical feminist resonance

I use my sisters
for whatever I can get

I use my sisters
as bed companions

I use my sisters
to write poems

I use my sister's
life as anti-capitalist poetic symbol

I use my sister's
fridge-chilled gin

I use my sisters'
free wine fundraisers

I have a lesbian
coterie out of nowhere
It just suddenly happened
like puberty or sex
ual preferences
& they've accepted me
as their disappointment
half-sister:

2.4 children can be mine without a turkey
baster

In the coffee house off
6th the brand name eats
away at the food:
roastown coffee
tossedtown salad
delicioustown soup
pushed the brand too fartown advertising

The thought of you
makes me so crazy
if I had Facebook©
you'd be my profile picture

Politics and art can't
always   align;
you can't always be ethical
in your aesthetics
otherwise we'd all love murals
wouldn't we?
But they're clumsy
one dimensional &
it's not as if Diego didn't cheat
on his wife anyway

& the MOMA costs me $8 entry
while where I come from oil
painting is egalitarian:
in my country art is free

in the tall glass of cold milk shaded rooms
there's a Pollock of people
in front of the Bacon
which is hung outside the cheese croissant
café
            the bodies no longer distorted flesh
            but a warning against cholesterol

Flesh is the reason oil painting was invented
De Kooning said
& Bacon developed technique
to be the symbol of American dietary problems

It looks like
the iPad© might
just be the

death of art; canvases
a multiple screen simulacrum
clicked and saved in 'gallery visits'
what would O'Hara think of
that? I mean, what do I? And if I do,
perhaps I am myself again

I pass Jasper John's
Flag
and see the pointed
left leg of the 16th
star stiletto angular
dancing out of America
out of line with its elegant   reach

Carl Andre   Robert Smithson
a pile of bricks   mirrored structure
          Where is Ana Mendieta?
In the spaces between
the masculine cutting
up land or erecting
structures
I expect to see her fallen over the two
so that her body
leaves its imprint on the land; this hard
grey for effect concrete floor
to see her outlined and indigenous in
the bricks of her husband

NY women everywhere pushed & jumping
these beautiful lofts are a health hazard

They say Francesca
Woodman was
impossible to
recognise

In the Frick
amongst all the paintings
of Jesus having a shit time
I see the *Polish Rider* with
its disparate horse and his
boy

its own Biarritz & San Sebastian
partly because of the horse's
breaking brushstroke forelegs

partly because in my bicycle-
for-two t-shirt my chest is
at least aspiring to some kind of love

partly because Frick made his
money through shooting workers
which is not our American dream

& it is hard to believe when I am with you that
there can be anything as still or as definitive as
the arts of the exploited or Remembrandts

bought with blood or collecting snuff
boxes from past times in glass cases
littered mosaic high aesthetic housing

and the portraits are nothing but paint & you
wonder how anyone could die for them

and I would rather look at the city than
anything else man-made
            because a woman could do
something here which is why I am telling you
about it
I think of you

(back home girls with
visible abs get
a lot of action
      good job they're flexible
which leaves them open
to interpretation)

and you have made me
so unsure of prepositions;
one look my way like
pulling the rug out
from over me

and I send a message to what seems like beyond
to say I don't know how I feel about beauty
boxes; the cubing of a face's possibility or the
collecting of trinkets delicate as ladies' fingers
when our hands are now rough with touching
one another & digging our way out

my hands are miner's hands
minder's hands; agitating the
Atlantic between you & I with
letters
      typed and written
with each nail a mild glamour of pollution
dusted & darkened under the top

In Madison Square
Gardens
I eat a tomato
biting hard into the
bleak red heart of
something unfathomable
& seeded flesh moving
under the pressure of
lip line watching the sky line
through leafing trees

the sexual act of eating
a tomato
this delicacy of fertility
in NY city where
I eat what I buy

or at least eat
what I can take
but this is no
clumsy consumption
sliced vegetable
but a roundness
a wholeness bitten
half-wild dark & open

It is 9:20 in New York a Wednesday
three days after Bastille day
and I am on my way to see a lesbian
who is happily a hasbian which is a trend
for women who have given up

on women which is also the contemporary
state of third waves which are becoming
like Reichs though I'm not allowed to
say that in front of Germans or feminists
not knowing which would take

greater offence. Being English in this
city today makes me a figure of fun
funnier figurative than in person as
a slip of colonial blondness but nonetheless
I am accented & accentuated by

the difference of my talk. And the
walk that doesn't fit my speech the
way it should were this a cowboy film
which it is not but I am ready for the
quick-draw under the stars & striped

10pm sky when the fireworks start.

and if I'm anybody's type I'd like to be a stereo
or if I'm your type I'd like to be a writer
of poetry, no LANGUAGE prototype &
he calls me Miss like I'm his type but
it might just be because he works at the
hotel & has to be polite to the girl

as he talks me through my name tells me
it is beautiful & he heard it only once before
on *Charmed*
where the character died after three seasons

MEDITATIONS ON THE LINE

I am always crossing lines
but I've tried to draw a line under it
put a line through that

Why made in sand not paper;
effaced by timeline & tideline?

I've started to replace line with trajectory in my
day-to-day parlance, which is how I have come to
think of the poem

highline skyline, try-line, by-line
deadline;
toeing it with one pen holding hand.

Line-breaks like break-ups
are immaterial if they make
high art

Being opposed to the line-dance
with partners; uniform, sequential
being in love with the
line dance;
an irreverence of feet

Walking the line
like London
like New York
I see you in the grid of my vision

spelling you out
on a cruise line
We eat oysters in the bar
at Grand Central Station
can't remember a single film

to re-enact now we're here.
Their ceiling is a constellation
for our meeting where Mars
almost collides in its painted

rush with Aries; until we're
confused & Roman & mystical
though we're not at all

and Liam Neeson will keep playing the
trained mentor
Morgan Freeman will keep playing the
wise janitor
Christian Bale will always be trapped in a
labour camp somewhere
& the woman will be interchangeable in her
red dress

and there is the same inevitability
in the shittiest bar
this side of town
hitting the letter roads of the
Lower East Side

The discordant
act of eating
a grilled tomato
cut
so it does not
resemble a
fruit

some cruder
in shape
than others
in the rush
to remove
harder bits

like stamens
a concentrated
area of growth
pulsing amber
at the centre of
the tomato

and then grilled.
The top not like
a kiss now
peeling back skin
to sensation

but held down
on a griddle pan

LYRIC POSSIBILITIES

*For I is other. If brass wakes as a bugle, it is not
its fault at all.*

Luckily, it's all about me:
no 'I' involved

Lyric tradition
became an
I-sore
a sight for sore I's

An idea is not ours and not alive unless it is
essentially an event or part of an episode in
human thinking, unless it occurs in a
subjectivity.

So now readable
beauty is in the I of the beholder
& me?
Maybe the apple of your I?

The I's are the mirror of the soul
& me – the
subjective glass –
couldn't be more transparent

though, never forget
in the kingdom of the blind
the one 'I' woman is King.

I am enamoured of the inadequacies
of your character

women figure even more prominently on any
list of contemporary poets for whom the New
York school influence has been decisive

it's got so that
I wonder what
we're all doing
sometimes

the New York School pursued an aesthetic
agenda that was deliberately apolitical, even
antipolitical.

put your hands
round my waist
like the neck
of a bottle

& let's forget these heavy implications of want

Acknowledgments

Eileen Myles 'The Lesbian Poet' in *School of Fish* (Black Sparrow, 1997) for inspiring '(Coteries.)'

Frank O'Hara's poems 'Mayakovsky', 'Having a Coke with You,' and 'The Day Lady Died' in *The Collected Poems of Frank O'Hara* ed. Donald Allen (University of California Press, 1995) informed the structure and content of 'A Voyage.'

All of the italicised sections of 'A Voyage' are taken from Daniel Kane's, *All Poets Welcome: The Lower East Side Poetry Scene in the 1960s* (University of California Press, 2003).

9 781912 211159